Kick Credit Card Debt Now!

New Ideas for Cutting Expenses and Becoming Debt-Free

Legal & Disclaimer

The author has made every effort to ensure the accuracy of the information within this book was correct at time of publication. The author does not assume and hereby disclaims any liability to any party for any loss, damage, or disruption caused by errors or omissions, whether such errors or omissions result from accident, negligence, or any o

Introduction

Are you deep in credit card debt with no way out that you can see? If you're a, shall we say, "spontaneous" shopper, or simply have a lot of bills you can't pay without the help of using credit cards for daily needs, you need to find a way out.

Here it is.

This e-book will help you attack credit card debt in ways that make sense and give you the maximum of results in the shortest amount of time. We'll set you on the path to success when it comes to killing off that nagging debt.

We offer not only the best ways to pay each card off, but what to do with them afterward – DON'T cut them up or it will harm your credit score! Just learn to use them more responsibly.

We'll also give you concrete ways to cut expenses in every aspect of your life, so you can be debt-free and ready to face the rest of your financial life as a downhill battle, instead of an uphill battle.

Chapter 1 – How did your Credit Card Balances get so High?

In 2010, households with credit card balances averaged more than $7,200 in debt. It's safe to assume that this average has only grown in the last five years. What's worse than the debt is the average interest rate these households are paying – a staggering 17% to 20%! These rates make it difficult for people to dig their way out of debt. Why does credit card debt grow so quickly?

Why Worry about Interest?

Interest is usually charged in APR, or annual percentage rate. This is the fee you pay for borrowing money to purchase what you want, when you want it, on a credit card. The interest allows you to spend money today instead of having to save the money over time and then spend it.

Interest is charged if you don't pay the full amount due every month on your credit cards. If you pay the full amount due each month, you will not generally be charged interest. The prime rate sometimes affects the rate you pay. This is the rate which the US Federal Reserve charges its highest rated customers. Some card issuers have variable rates, while others have rates that remain the same.

Different card issuers have different interest rates, and often these are based on your credit score. You may have a rate that is higher or lower than neighbours, friends or family members. When you pay your credit card bills on time every month, you'll build a stronger credit score and this will help in increasing your ability to become qualified for credit cards that have lower APRs.

Credit card issuers must give you 45 days or more notice if they are changing your interest rate, or making other specific changes. The higher interest rate, if yours increases, only applies to transactions that occur after the change. Most credit card companies re-evaluate interest increases every six months. If they are trimming rates, they will also be reduced with a 45 day written notice.

As a consumer, you have the right to refuse or opt out of some changes to your terms. This is not the case with changes in your APR. If you decide to refuse acceptance of certain changes in terms, this usually leads to your account being cancelled.

Keep your eye on the cumulative interest charged to you on your credit card statements. This can get you into trouble if you don't follow it. Unless you pay your balance in full every month, interest fees can add up and you may not realize how much more in debt you're becoming, if you don't keep your eye on it.

As an example, if you have a $5,000 balance on a credit card and it has a 20% rate of interest, the annual interest charged will be $1,000. You may pay thousands in credit card interest every year if you don't watch your credit card spending. This puts you further in debt.

Credit Card Fees really Add Up

You'll be a more responsible card holder if you understand how the fees work with each issuer. Read your new card member agreement when you get a card and file it in a place where you can easily refer to it.

The most common fees include:

- Cash advance fees

- Balance transfer fees

- Fees for airline miles cards

- Fees for rewards cards

- Foreign currency conversion fees if you're out of the United States

- Fees for using out-of-network ATMs

- Fees for extra copies of monthly statements

- Late fees

- Returned check fees

Companies that issue credit cards charge various fees that allow them to earn more of a profit. Some cards have annual fees even if you don't use the cards. Others will charge a fee if you go over the limit for credit on their cards. If you are late on a payment or miss one, that will usually add to your fees.

If you transfer a balance from one card to another, especially if this is done in a promotional period with a low interest lure, you may be charged a fee that is equal to some percentage of what you are transferring. Check your statements to determine if you are being charged extra fees.

Your monthly credit card statement shows your ending balance from the last cycle, all charges and payments you have made during the month and any fees and interest that were added to your credit card balance.

If you have been charged an over limit or late fee and it's the first time you've had one, call your credit card company. If you have had a good previous payment history with them, they may waive the fee as a courtesy.

Breakdown of Credit Card Fees

If you don't pay the minimum amount due by

the date it is due, you'll be charged a late fee. This fee can increase if you make more late payments. Your late payment fee is not usually larger than the minimum payment due.

If your payment is not paid by your bank (if you bounce a check) there is a returned check fee. It's ironic that the people who incur these fees are the ones who can least afford them, but that's how the system works. Additional returned checks may cause higher fees, after your first one.

Drowning in Credit Card Debt?

Debt on credit cards accounts for a large chunk of the total consumer debt owed in the United States. Credit cards can be important for your day to day life, unless you don't use them or can't get them. It's important that you understand the money it will cost you to carry credit card debt, unless you pay your cards off each month.

If you have $2,000 in debt on your credit card and a minimum payment due each month of $10, and you pay extra on top of that, it will help you to pay less in interest fees. If you only pay the minimum amount due each month, you will be paying more in interest.

If you pay off your card at the minimum payment and don't ever use it again, it will cost you $4240 over 15 years to pay off the $2,000 you charged on the card. If, on the other hand, you paid an extra $10 each month, your total paid would be $3276 and it would only take you seven years to pay off your card balance. Paying just $10 extra each month saves you nearly $1,000 in interest fees and cuts your period of repayment by over seven years!

There is a lesson to be learned here and that is that even paying a little bit extra will help you. Paying twice the minimum amount due or even more will cut down drastically on the interest you pay and the time it takes to pay off the debt.

It's better, of course, to pay off your credit cards in full each month, so you don't carry a balance, but this is not always possible.

Saving is like Earning

Let's say your credit cards have a 20% interest rate on them. If you invest, you would likely be quite happy to receive yearly returns of 20% on your investments. But if someone told you that a stock offered that rate of return, you would be rightly skeptical.

However, if you pay off your credit card balance every month, you save 20% in interest, which is just the same as getting a 20% return on an investment.

Paying off Debt is a Good Investment

You may be reluctant to pay your credit cards off each month, and decide to put some money in savings accounts or investments, instead. It's natural to want to have money in savings for a rainy day, or in investments for your retirement.

Remember, though, that $1 is always $1, whether you're losing it or investing it. Putting $10 in savings at 4% interest paid and not paying it instead on a credit card that charges $20 interest is losing money. Leaving a balance due on your credit cards negates gains you make in investments, unless you're making over 20% on your investments, and that generally doesn't happen.

When you pay off your credit cards with the extra money you have each month, you're guaranteeing yourself a return on your investment of whatever percentage of interest the card company charges. After you pay off credit cards, you'll have more spending or investment money, since you're not paying interest. Then your investments can grow.

Credit Card Management

Charging things on your credit cards is not the only aspect of being a credit card holder. The other is paying the card issuers back. If you'd prefer not to be among the many Americans who have ruined their credit score with credit cards, learn more about them. If you are not understanding what your credit limits or high balances mean, your credit score could tank, which makes it difficult to get a mortgage, other types of loans or potentially even a job.

Credit Limits

Your credit limit is the maximum amount you can spend on a card. It is established by each credit card company. Your income and credit score will determine what type of credit limits you'll be able to get. When you get your cards, each issuer will keep tabs on the way it is used. It's important to pay bills on time. They will also check whether you use the card for cash advances and whether you are routinely paying off your full balance every month. Credit limits can be lowered or raised, depending on what your credit history looks like.

Lowering or Raising Credit Limits

Your credit card company may be willing to raise your credit limit if you ask them. If you pay bills on time, it can happen. If you have a better job, and higher income, your chances are even better to have a credit limit raised.

Credit card issuers also sometimes reduce credit limits. Reasons for this include a lower credit score, maxing out the card (hitting or going over your limit) or making late payments. Sometimes credit card companies lower credit limits for an entire group of customers, and it may not have anything to do with something you did.

High(est) Balance

This term refers to your highest amount owed on a credit card. It factors into your overall credit score, too. If you want to gain a higher credit score, your credit card balance should not go over 1/3 of your limit.

The amount of credit you have available to use is relevant in determining your credit score. Your FICO score is important. It's a scoring system used by credit reporting agencies to determine whether you are a good risk for new credit.

Negative Credit Consequences

Be sure you're aware of your credit limits and how much you charge each month. You don't want to go over your available credit. This can not only lead to fees for being over your limit; it can also increase your interest rate for using the card. If you go over the limit too many times, the issuer can close that account.

Use Credit Correctly

If you use credit cards and other credit sources properly, it keeps you from getting in hot water financially, and helps you in building a stronger credit history. This will allow you to get better deals if you need loans. Even one mistake with a credit card can haunt your credit report for years, since businesses routinely share credit histories. When you understand the principal and interest/fees, you will be better equipped to build and then maintain creditworthiness in the short and long term.

Track your Principal

Your principal is the amount of money you have charged, transferred or advanced to yourself on a credit card. If you make a purchase, that becomes part of the balance on your credit card, and this is the principal on which the issuer charges interest.

Likewise, if you transfer balance from other credit cards or get money at an ATM with your credit card, this is principal, too.

The best option is charging only things you need on your credit cards. Read the credit card agreement to check the different interest rates charged for different types of principal. Transfers sometimes have an interest-free period, but most charges will be charged interest after the first month. Cash advances may have higher interest rates. If you pay late or miss a payment, interest rates can increase and progressively skyrocket.

Credit Tricks and Tips

You don't have to accept pre-approved credit card "deals" that are sent to you. Shop for the lowest interest rates before you decide on what card(s) you want. Some credit unions or other businesses offer you a card with no annual fee and lower interest rates. They may forgive some of the late fees other issuers charge, and offer low interest rates and better grace periods.

Every time you apply for a credit card, your credit score will be temporarily lowered, so be picky. Once you do get a card, signing up for online payments is a good idea, so you won't miss any. Missed payments can be reported to the credit reporting agencies, and this information is available to other lenders.

Chapter 2 – Pay off those Credit Cards ASAP

On your credit card statements, there is a minimum payment due listed. This can be quite enticing – you're only paying a small amount and for awhile anyway, you don't have to worry about the entire bill. Unfortunately, paying the minimum payment on credit card(s) will generally haunt you in the long term.

As an example, if you owe about $15,000 on your credit cards and pay the minimum amount due on each card every month, you will pay over $11,000 in total interest before the bills are paid off.

Paying the Minimum Amount Due doesn't Help You

There are sometimes good reasons for running up debt on credit cards. Perhaps you had an illness, lost your job or had expensive car repairs that you didn't expect. Regardless of what causes the expenditures, you need to rid yourself of credit card debt as your top priority, financially.

Speak with an expert, if you need to, and develop an action plan that will help you to reduce and eliminate – eventually – your credit card debt. You can also create an action plan on your own, if you understand how credit cards, interest rates and fees work.

Credit Card Payment Action Plans

1. Request that your creditors give you a lower rate of interest. Sometimes it just takes a few phone calls to get reduced rates for your credit cards. You will need to have a credit score of 720 or higher, as a rule, to get your APR lowered. You should also make all your payments on time and be a long-term cardholder.

If you have been offered any lower APR by a competitor, you can bring that up to the customer service representative. They will sometimes match the other offer, if they want to keep you as a customer.

2. You may decide to target the credit card

with the smallest balance to pay off first. If you have balances on a number of cards, wiping out that debt can be slow going. It will help you to feel motivated if you can pay one off first. It gives you a target that you can shoot for that will come sooner than your eventual goal of getting rid of all your credit card debt.

Paying the smallest card first shows more progress every month, which may keep you more motivated. This snowball strategy pays off the smallest balance first, and when that is done, the next smallest. The extra money will "snowball", and will eventually overpower the amount of debt on your highest balance.

It's true that you'll pay more interest when you pay the smaller bills first. But if you need more motivation, this method has behavioural and psychological value. You'll feel good when you see a zero balance on a credit card account. This may be a better motivator to stay with the plan and eventually become debt-free.

While logic dictates paying the card with the highest interest rate or highest balance first, short term goals can be important. Your credit card that has the highest rate may not also have the lowest balance. Be aware that you will pay more in interest if you pay the smallest balances off first.

3.   Focusing on the credit card that has the highest interest rate is another way to go. This will save you the most money, but it won't necessarily keep you as motivated as paying off a little balance card first.

This does make sense. Higher interest rates will generally cause you more financial pain. If you're only paying $40 or $50 a month on a high balance, high interest credit card, you're paying more in interest and taking longer to pay it off.

If you focus on the highest interest card, while still making minimum payments or more on the other cards you have, the next move after the highest is paid off is to go to the next highest interest rate card. Pursue this until you have eliminated your debt.

This is a very responsible way to pay debt, but it may seem slow. If you have a lot of credit card debt, you may become overwhelmed that you're not paying your cards off sooner. Don't continue to use cards if you can avoid it, since that's just adding to the problem.

4.   Consider a balance transfer. Do this only with caution. Moving a balance owed from a higher-interest card to one with lower interest can save you a lot of money. However, you must be committed to paying off that debt before the introductory window of low interest rates is over. This usually lasts between a year and 18 months.

You must make your payments on time on the transferred balance, too. Otherwise that rate can skyrocket, and could even end up higher than the account you transferred the balance from.

Don't make large purchases with the new card, either, unless you must. The low introductory rate often will only apply to balance transfers and not new purchases. You will usually have to pay a fee for a balance transfer, too, which runs about three to four percent of the amount you are transferring.

5.   Look into peer-to-peer lending. If you can't pay off your credit card balance in full, so that you're

clear of the debt, consider borrowing some money to pay it off, from peer-to-peer lenders at sites like Prosper.com or LendingClub.com. They offer loans whose fixed rates of interest can be 20-30% less than credit cards. This can save you hundreds in interest. If you have a good credit score and a secure job, you may be able to request an online loan for up to roughly $25,000.

6. If you are truly strapped for cash, just try to make two payments on each card per month (each one equivalent to at least the minimum amount due). Credit cards are often charged interest daily, so earlier payments can mean a faster reduction in your overall debt. This means that you'll pay less in interest, too.

Make the minimum payment before the due date and try to pay the same amount about two weeks later. You can pay double the minimum every month until you pay off the credit card debt. This is slower than paying higher amounts, but at least you're doing something to help pay down your debt.

Remind yourself with sticky notes or on your phone calendar to make that extra payment each month. Want to know what a difference it makes? If you have a $2,000 balance on a 17% APR card, paying the minimum only will take you more than 20 YEARS to pay off the debt. Paying the minimum twice a month will have the card paid off in less than just three years!

7.   You can also elect to set a target between highest and lowest. If you can pay a certain amount on three or four different cards, you can pay the same on each one, if it motivates you. Be sure that you make at least your minimum payments and that you are paying more than just the finance charge. Your finance charge will make up accrued interest every month if you don't pay off cards in full by their due date. If your minimum payment is less than their finance charges, and you only pay the minimum, you're actually paying interest ON the interest! That's not a good thing.

The method that works best for you depends on how you are wired and which strategy keeps you motivated to pay off your debt. Remember, though that the strategy is more important than just feeling good about paying. Pay all your credit card bills early or on time. Late fees can not only add to your original debt, but they can cause the credit card issuer to raise your interest rates.

You are not Alone

We're not talking aliens among us here. We're just letting you know that you are certainly not the only one who pays a large chunk of change on credit cards every month. About 40% of Americans have a credit card balance on one or more cards, says a study conducted in 2012.

Digging your way out of credit card debt may be intimidating and frustrating, but if you can do it, you'll be so much better off, financially.

Understand how you got this deep in debt to start with. Home repairs and medical emergencies do happen. But compulsive shopping and charging things you don't really need can accumulate so that your credit card debt becomes almost unmanageable.

Helping your Credit Score

Understand what you are eligible for when you're planning to pay off your credit card debt. Your credit score plays a huge role in what you can and cannot do. If your credit is bad, you won't qualify for things like competitive personal loans or balance transfers.

If your credit score is lower than 600, this makes it difficult to qualify for personal loans and balance transfer offers. Once you get above 680, this will open the door to more options and SOME balance transfer offers. After you get up to 720 or above, you can utilize any of the best methods to help in reducing debt.

More Helpful Tips in Paying off Debt

Create a Workable Budget

Establishing a budget is the first major step in solving your problem with debt. There are online programs that can help, or you can just use an Excel spreadsheet or a piece of paper.

Include monthly income and your expenses, as well. Check over your categories within the budget where costs can be cut. The longer you don't cut back on your spending, the deeper your hole of debt will become.

Delete your Credit Card Information at online Sites

If you shop online a lot, you may have a stored credit card at your favorite shopping sites. This does make it easier to checkout, and that's the problem. It makes it easier to buy things that you don't really need. Clear your credit card information out of your favorite stores, so you'll have to enter the information manually. If you pay for recurring services, use a credit card service debit card that is linked to just your checking account.

Deleting credit card information is also a very prudent step in avoiding identity theft and the chance that hackers can gain access to your credit information from online sites.

Got a Bonus? Target Debt with it

If your company gives you a bonus, whether it's during the holidays or at another time of year, allocate the money toward paying off your debt. It's tempting to spend bonuses on frivolous things or vacations, but that's not the wisest way to spend the money. Your financial situation is more important than buying a Coach handbag.

Change your Daily Routines

Your habits each day are the main reason you're in debt. Think about the ways in which you spend money on a daily basis. Then think about each week and month. Do you need that gourmet coffee every morning? Can you pack a lunch instead of going out? Ask yourself: What can you change every day without having to sacrifice your lifestyle?

Have you Reached a Milestone? Reward Yourself

Paying down your debt is not a punishment,

and it won't be paid off any quicker even if you view it that way. You have to keep at it every day, and in order for that to happen, you have to be motivated.

Your reward should not be a week's trip to a spa or resort. That's an unreasonable expenditure, even for a reward. How about a camping trip over the weekend? If you have reduced your credit card debt as much as you targeted for the month or year, pat yourself on the back. It's not easy to get out of credit card debt.

Bonus Tips

Check out these tips. They will help you stop spending money elsewhere so that you can use it to pay off your credit card debt.

1.   Take stock of your liabilities. They let you know just how much you owe on credit cards and other loans. Enter them in a spreadsheet and list your monthly payments, amounts due in interest, account balances and a total of all your account balances. Update it as you are able to pay debt off, and watch

the total go down. It will motivate you to keep working towards your goal.

2. Build an emergency fund. Whenever you have extra money coming in, like a tax refund, etc, add it to the emergency fund and then pay off debt.

OR

3. Keep one credit card for emergencies. Otherwise keep the account balance low, and pay off the balance every month, when you can.

4. Be firm with yourself and your spending. Make it a commitment and revisit it whenever you notice you're not making headway on your debt. Change is not easy and you'll need a drastic mindset change to get out of credit card debt. You CAN do it, as long as you truly want to.

5. Praise yourself and your family for every accomplishment. This does NOT mean spending money frivolously. Do something rewarding that's not expensive, like a free movie at the local cinema center.

6. Change. This means change yourself, your spouse and your family. Whoever is the biggest

spender will be the hardest to change. Change your own attitude and spending behaviors first and help your family to follow.

7.   Be realistic and honest with yourself. If the debt has been accumulating for four or five years, it will take longer than that to get out.

8.   Make sure your budget is realistic, too. Put any money that you can toward paying off your debt. Allow occasional recreational or social activities, as long as they are not expensive.

9.   Be patient. Paying off debt takes time. Depending on what method you decide to use, you may not see much progress, at first. It will still happen.

10. Track expenses closely. Use software like Quicken. Put your expenses in categories and record the amount you spend in every category, so that problems are easier to spot. Target those areas for reduction.

11. Leave yourself and your family just a bit of wiggle room. Life will throw you unexpected expenses

at times. Include slack in your payoff plans, to handle the setbacks.

12. Keep your eyes on the long-term goal. See where you will be in five or ten years.

13. Find a true purpose. Is it starting a business, working from home, or sending your children to college? It will drive your passion to find motivation beyond money. Otherwise, you won't be as driven. Passion helps you do the right things, like halting credit card use. Take a look at what you value most deeply and judge your actions by that framework.

14. Are you getting a raise? Funnel the extra money into paying off debt.

15. Focus, focus, focus on debt and on getting out of it. Living on credit will always get you in trouble.

16. Change the ways you think about money. How much do you net per hour? This can be figured out whether you are on a salary or an hourly worker, or even if you own your own company. Apply the time

to any purchase you want to make. Is that new 60" flat screen TV worth 20-30 hours of time? Seeing spending in hours instead of dollars can help you change your spending habits more quickly.

17. Spend money on your goals. If you want to have more money to have children and allow you or your spouse to quit work and stay home with them, then cut back on entertainment and clothes, etc. Don't spend money on things you don't really care about.

18. Keep wealth in mind rather than debt. If you're focusing on getting out of debt, then all you're thinking about is debt. If you're thinking that your current situation will lead to your overall wealth, this will keep you saving.

19. Keep positive thoughts in mind. It's hard to say "no" to yourself all the time. Instead of thinking that way, see the money you owe getting lower every month.

20. Don't sweat the sacrifices. You own things, not the other way around. Saving money in other areas to pay off debt is empowering.

21. Educate your family. Teach the children not to make the same mistakes you and your spouse have made, with regards to debt.

Chapter 3 – Raise Your Credit Score & other Strategies to Become Debt-Free

Raise your Credit Score

Most people don't realize that it is possible to make a dent in your credit score in a relatively short period of time. "Short" may not mean what you want it to mean, though. It can take between one and two months or more to boost that number that holds more power every day over your life.

Here are some positive steps to take in that direction:

1. Get a Credit Card

This just means getting one, not using it whenever something strikes your eye. Having cards that you use only occasionally and then pay off looks good on your credit score. You have to be responsible with them and pay your bills in a timely manner.

If you cannot get a conventional credit card, sign up for a secured card. This is essentially borrowing your own money, but if you select one from a card issuer who reports to all three credit reporting agencies, you can give your credit score a boost.

2. Don't Use your Cards much

Get credit however you can, but don't use it when paying for everything you buy. Your cards should have no more than 30% of their available credit being used in order to be assets on your credit report.

3. Negotiate with your Creditors

You cannot deny it if you didn't pay on your credit card when you were sick and in the hospital two years ago. But some creditors will "erase" that debt, if you ask. Write the card issuer a letter in which you offer to pay the balance due if the creditor will simply report your account "paid as agreed". They may even agree to remove the entry from your credit report. Get it in writing before you pay.

Some creditors may also be open to goodwill adjustments. If you were a very good payer of bills before you were laid up in the hospital, write the card issuer a letter, pointing out how good your older history was and ask if the account can be removed from your report.

4. Check your Credit Limits

Be sure that the limits on your actual accounts are correctly reflected in your credit report. It shouldn't look like you're maxing a card out every month.

5. Ask your Creditor to Raise your Limit

This step makes your available credit look better, but ONLY if you don't use the extra availability opened up to you. If you can't be trusted not to charge right up to the maximum limit, don't request a higher limit. (You probably wouldn't get one, anyway, if your account is always close to being maxed out.)

Even if you pay off cards, don't close them. That would make your available credit lower. This doesn't look good to the credit bureaus. You can use an otherwise unused card for a routine bill, that you will pay off every month.

6. Become an Authorized User

If you can't get a credit card, you can ask a friend or relative to add you to his or her credit account. S/he may say "no" if you have a poor credit history, but if this person doesn't have a credit history yet, they may be willing to take a chance on you.

Put in writing your agreement on how much you will spend and pay. Use the card only when needed, and pay your share of the bills. Be a responsible card-holder.

7. Pay all your Bills on Time

The history of your account payments makes up more than 1/3 of your FICO score. If you are overwhelmed or forget things, get auto-payment for your bills, so you know they'll be paid on time. Watch your checking account balance to be sure you have enough to cover your automatic payments every month.

8. Use Different Types of Credit

To boost your credit modestly, use various types of credit. You could take out a small loan from your credit union or purchase an appliance or home furnishings on an installment loan. Only do so if you know you can pay them back properly.

Reporting Errors on your Credit Report

5% of people have credit report errors from lenders or credit bureaus, according to a recent FTC study. Mistakes do happen. You can dispute credit report errors through TransUnion, Equifax and Experian, and it can be done online.

Errors may end up on your report when banks, lenders or credit reporting agencies get something wrong. However, it's your job to find them and have them fixed. Credit bureaus do not have any obligation to correct errors unless you report something that is wrong.

Check your credit report on a regular basis. You can get one report free from each credit reporting agency per year. This means you can get a report each quarter, one from each credit bureau. The only place to get these free reports is at annualcreditreport.com.

When you get your reports, scan them closely

for any errors. Mis-spelled addresses or variations in your name don't matter quite as much. The serious mistakes to look for are accounts or collections that are not yours, late payments that actually weren't late and inquiries for loans that were not authorized by you.

If you find something that is inaccurate, dispute it with the credit reporting agency. If you find the same mistake on each bureau report, you must file the dispute with all three bureaus.

Here are some good Practices in Handling Disputes:

Often, snail mail correspondence works better when you deal with disputes, etc on your credit report. You can upload documents when you file a dispute online, but the form has a list of reasons you might be filing a dispute, and they may not exactly describe the problem you're reporting.

The Federal trade Commission (FTC) has a template letter that can be used in explaining your dispute. TransUnion and Equifax require that you also use their own dispute form when you contact them.

Be very clear when you are explaining errors on your credit report. It's not enough to tell them something isn't right. You need to present the facts that tell how and why the information is wrong. If you have more than one issue, include an itemized list. The person dealing with your dispute knows nothing about you, so approach your dispute with that in mind.

Prove your Claim

Give proof of your claim. You must substantiate any claim in whatever way will express it clearly. You must prove that you are right about their error. Find any paperwork that will help to support your case, like letters, identification, court documents and payment records.

As an example, if you have a loan payment that shows as late on your credit report, but you have your monthly statement that shows the payment was made on time, include a copy of that statement and highlight or circle the pertinent information. Never send original statements. Keep those for your own records.

Be sure that everything is documented. Before you mail your dispute paperwork, make copies of everything. Make a record of conversations you may have had with lenders, credit bureaus or banks. A paper trail will help you if you take legal action at a later date.

When you mail your dispute paperwork, send it via certified mail and attach a return receipt request so you know it has been received by the credit bureau.

Don't be worried if it takes a month or longer for the credit agencies to get in touch with you. They must look into the claim. Straighten things out well before you need to get a loan for anything, since the corrections will not usually be made quickly.

When the credit bureaus get back to you, their response will notify you whether your disputed item has been fixed, deleted or left unchanged. They will contact the lender and make sure that their records show the proper information.

If you have difficulty getting a dispute resolved,

it may be because:

•   The lender or bank is disagreeing with your claim. If you dispute an account that you do not recognize, and the lender agrees, it will come off your record. However, if they say the account is yours, that means it will usually stay on your credit report.

•   Your dispute does not have sufficient explanation or proof. If this happens to you and you think perhaps you can offer a case that is stronger, you may file another dispute. You can file as many times as you like even about one item you dispute, but if you don't provide more information to back up your claim, they may see your actions as being frivolous and ignore your request.

•   They have your account confused with another person's account. There may be similar names or social security numbers. The lender is unable to clear it up if it's the reporting agency's fault. If you think these errors might be a signal that someone is trying to steal your identity, contact the credit bureaus immediately and have them place a fraud alert on your credit file. This will limit any more damage from occurring.

All reports of problems should begin with a credit bureau dispute. This is a necessary step, especially if you ultimately determine that you will take legal action. You can also send your dispute claim to the lender or bank that made the mistake. Use the FTC sample letter and include documentation. If they do agree with your information, they must send corrected information to the credit reporting agencies.

A complaint can also be filed with the Consumer Financial Protection Bureau (CFPB). Credit bureaus must respond to these complaints since the CFPB regulates the agencies. This may urge them to fix the problem more quickly.

If you are still not seeing the errors corrected, you may opt for hiring an attorney who specializes in working with the Fair Credit Reporting Act. This person will sue the lender and credit bureau on your behalf. This is a costly step, so if the disputed item is not important, you can just let it go.

Raising your Credit Score

Most everyone has needed another chance at some point in their life. It's easier to use prepaid debit cards today, offering the simplicity of credit cards, but they won't help your score. If you want to purchase a car or a house, you will learn very quickly how important good credit is. If you have no credit or poor credit, you will probably be turned down for loans, or offered a loan with a sky-high interest rate.

Secured credit cards can help in these instances. They are tools to practice with and to demonstrate that you have the skills needed to use an unsecured credit card responsibly. Secured credit cards usually require a deposit from you in cash, for which you are granted a credit line. The amount you put down will determine your credit line.

This money is NOT used to pay your credit card bills after you have used the card. The first deposit to get the card is the bank's guarantee that it won't get burned if you don't pay your credit card bills.

Make Sure Payments will be Reported to the Credit Bureaus

Most secured card issuers report payments to the three credit bureaus, so if you pay your bill in a timely manner and follow the conditions and terms of your card, this can boost your credit score, over time. Secured cards are valuable tools, as long as you pay your bill on time.

There are some red flags to look out for when you are seeking a secured card. Be sure that your payments will be reported to the credit bureaus. If they aren't, then using that card is a waste of time. Fees vary from one issuer to the next, too.

Secured cards may have fees that are higher than unsecured cards, and there may be a difference in maintenance fees and interest rates, too. If you close the account and have no balance owed, you should make sure that you can get your initial deposit back without a long delay.

Avoid secured cards that don't offer you a grace period for payments. If they don't, you'll pay interest as soon as you swipe the card at a store. If you have a grace period, you can avoid paying interest by paying the full amount due each month. Watch for limitations placed on secured cards, too.

Don't Be Afraid of Secured Cards

These cautions are not meant to effectively scare you away from using secured cards to help in rebuilding your credit. As long as you're aware of the issues like reporting to the credit bureaus, secured cards can help to get you back on track.

Credit Scores and the Latest Recession

If you have a lower than ideal credit score, you can feel a bit better if you realize that many people have had this problem since the recession in 2008. Credit scores were hit hard. However, you need a good score to get not only loans but also reasonable insurance quotes.

Tips to help you Rebuild a Good Credit Score

1. Catch up on payments you have missed. If

you are having problems in making your payments, speak to your creditors or have a not-for-profit credit counsellor negotiate payments for you.

2.   Be sure that you pay all your bills on time from now on. This is the biggest factor used when your credit score is calculated. Companies with whom you have dealt successfully may also be willing to write letters of recommendation when you are applying for credit.

3.   Use automatic payments if you don't already. This will ensure that your bills are paid on time. One huge caveat here is not to overdraw your account.

4.   If you miss any payments, contact your creditors as soon as you can and ask if they can remove late payments from your credit record. Some will, just as a courtesy, especially if you have been a good customer up til now.

5.   The next most heavily weighted factor in determining your credit score after payment history is how much credit you use. Pay down cards whenever you can, so that you have available credit showing on

them.

6.   Don't close credit cards you've had for years. This may impact your credit score negatively. This is because your credit history length is important. If you want to get rid of a card with an annual fee, instead ask the creditor to switch your card to one that does not have fees.

7.   If you don't have credit yet, that's a different problem. You have to have credit to build good credit. Opening a secured card (see above) is easier than getting an unsecured card, but you could still need the help of a co-signer, to get approved.

8.   After you make payments on time for several months, ask your bank or lender to upgrade you to an unsecured credit card. You might wish to start with department store credit cards, since they are generally easier to get. If you pay your balance in full every month for six months to a year, you can try then to apply for a regular credit card from a bank.

9.   Don't apply for every card offer you receive. Inquiries for new credit may be damaging to your credit score, too. Searching for the single best loan is

more favourably looked upon than applying for a number of new credit lines.

Strategies for a Debt-Free Life

You might think it's impossible, but there are plenty of consumers who live without running up debt. Whatever your age and income level, you can make that a choice. It's certainly not easy, but don't allow unbelievers to dissuade you, if you want to try.

Some people who are especially dedicated to saving money even go on spending diets, where they set limits on how much can be spent on each want or need. There are many methods you can use to cut spending and pay back your debt, and then avoid getting in debt. You need to choose a system that will work for you. You are the best judge of your own weaknesses, so choose your methods accordingly.

Making Lifestyle Changes

If you want to stay out of debt and avoid late fees and collections, there are lifestyle choices you can make to help you avoid getting into debt. It requires a great deal of discipline, but you will find it worth the trouble since you won't be wasting money on interest payments. Even if you've been deeply in debt, you can get out and stay out, going forward.

Strategies to avoid debt:

1. Pay off your credit card transactions right away

You don't have to use cash only, to avoid getting into debt. Using physical currency does make it easier to see where your money is going, and to make it impossible to run up a big debt from credit cards.

Credit cards make some transactions easier, though. If you're making reservations at a hotel or renting a car, credit cards are easier than cash, but most businesses will take debit cards, even though they may charge your card immediately for the full amount.

If you know you can't handle a credit card without using it for spur-of-the-moment purchases, don't choose credit cards as an option for you. If you can use them wisely, credit cards are handy for cash back or reward points.

If you do use your credit card regularly, you can pay off each purchase on the day it was made. Don't wait for your monthly bill to arrive. This forces you to think about the amount of money you have available for purchases before you pull out the plastic.

2. Rent a Home until you have Money to Buy a House

To many people, renting for an extended period of time may seem like a nightmare. However, real estate is expensive. Housing is the biggest challenge to living debt-free. If you rent in an area that is not over-priced, you can save up enough money to purchase a modest home. It may take a long time, but saving for years while renting can bring you an ultimate reward.

Renting does have its own frustrations and challenges, but not all landlords are greedy or inattentive, and you'll find renter's insurance is quite affordable. If you are not married and cannot afford living alone, you might rent out a room or sublet until you find a cheaper place to rent.

3.   Build up your Savings

If you work toward having a sizable amount in savings, you'll find it difficult, but it is the main ingredient that keeps you out of debt. Your savings prepare you for any unexpected expenses. When car repairs or medical expenses pop up, you will have the money to pay them, instead of charging them.

Saving is an essential element of handling long-term expenses too, like purchasing a home or financing a child's education. Savings can be enjoyed too, for well-deserved vacations.

Keeping a high savings balance will help you avoid needing credit for the unexpected expenses that occur in everyone's life. If you live without any loans, this cuts out many monthly payments taken on by other consumers. This creates more room in your personal budget for savings.

4.   Buy an inexpensive Used Car

There aren't many Americans in the middle class who can afford to purchase new cars with cash, so most of them get loans for the purpose. You don't need a car loan. You can find a reliable used auto.

There is always risk when you buy a pre-owned car, but if you do your research, check the CARFAX reports and take a car to your mechanic before buying, you can find a reliable car. Maintenance and repair costs will likely not be anywhere near as high as car payments.

You can use public transportation, if you live in town. Carpools are a good choice if you live near people who work in the same area as you do. If you live in a rural area, you may not have a choice other than getting a dependable, used vehicle.

Purchase a fuel-efficient vehicle if you need a car. It will save you lots of money in the long run. If you drive your vehicle for 80 thousand miles and the car you choose gets 25 miles per gallon of gas, rather than choosing one that gets 15 miles per gallon, it will save you over $6,000 over that 80,000 miles.

Research fuel-efficient driving, too. No hot-rodding. Drive sensibly and safely.

5. Higher Education Goals? Attend Community Colleges

Every year, students take out loans to attend college. You don't need to borrow money in order to get a good education. You can start out at local community colleges to finish some of your coursework there, before heading to a university that is more prestigious.

Grants and scholarships are also very helpful when you are attending college. Some students will have to eventually take out student loans, but if you have taught yourself how to save money instead of spending it, you may be able to work your way through college as you can afford classes.

6. Only Buy what you Need

If you're an impulse shopper, this will not be an attractive strategy. It is truly amazing how much money you can save by thinking before you make a purchase. Think well in advance of what you need, and budget for it.

Spend time researching the best possible deals and only buy things that you actually need. This doesn't mean living off the grid. It means spending the money you need to spend in order to live, but having fun without spending a lot of money.

It is difficult at first to stick to this rule, but if you practice, it will become easier. If you need stricter guidelines to save money within this strategy, budget your funds on paper and set goals that are financially reasonable.

Chapter 4 – Other Ways to Dave Money & Pay off Credit Card Debt

Cut Costs and Pay off Credit Cards Faster

The solution to paying down your credit card bills doesn't always involve shopping for other credit cards or loans. You can cut your expenses to free up more money. Even your smallest bills will add up, and each one drains your resources.

How to Save on Debt

Reducing your amount owed means lowering your monthly expenses. Here are some concrete ways to cut down on debt and reduce expenses, to free up money to use in paying down your credit card debt.

1. Consolidating your Student Loans

Some of these loans come with hefty interest rates. If you consolidate them, this can free up money to pay on credit cards.

2. Lowering your Costs for Energy

Heating and cooling your home and powering all of your high-tech devices and your big-screen TV can be pricey. You can improve your house's energy efficiency and pay less for utilities so that you can earmark that money to pay down debt.

Your hot water heater uses a lot of energy, and the conventional types are very inefficient. Why should you pay to keep 50 gallons of water hot all the time, when you only use it for showers and laundry?

Drop the temperature on your hot water heater and put a water heater blanket on it, to keep heat from escaping. Insulate any pipes that happen to be exposed. If you can afford it, invest in point-of-use heat-on-demand water heaters. They only heat the water when you need it.

Unplugging things when you're not using them will save money on your utility bills. It may not be a lot, but every little bit adds up. Using power strips is a good idea, and timers that turn things off when they are not being used.

CFL light bulbs or LED bulbs are just about four times more efficient than those old bulbs you used to use. The LEDs and CFLs last for years. Even if you decide to just change the bulbs you use the most, this can save you almost $50 a year on your electric bill!

3. Refinancing a Car or House

Ask at lending institutions to see if you can refinance a car or a house. The HARP program, for example, may allow you to refinance your home even if you're underwater in your mortgage. Locking in a lower rate will reduce bills and save money.

4. Stop Collecting

Do you have old beanie babies or Longaberger baskets you thought would make you rich? How did that work out for you? Don't collect things unless you know through research that they will hold their value. Even if your old collectibles aren't worth what you thought they would be, they may still have value. Sell them if you can and use the funds to pay down credit card debt.

5. Saving Bucks on Food

There are lots of ways to save money at the

grocery store. It's so easy to go over your budget in buying food, since prices vary a lot. You can purchase generic brands of food and other types of products and save a bundle. Check the ingredients lists, to make sure the generic products are actually similar to the name brands.

You might want to try purchasing non-perishable foods in bulk sizes. They aren't always a bargain, so check the price per ounce. Using coupons helps, too.

Eat at home more, instead of eating out or grabbing fast food. If you're busy – and we all are – consider cooking meals a day or two before you need them and then freezing them.

Gardening can help you save money, and it's a great way to be earth-friendly and eat healthy produce. You know it's healthy if you grew it yourself. Store (can/jar) excess veggies and use them whenever you need them.

Prepare lunches for school and work, at home. Be sure you only use foods that are easy to store, and that will remain fresh and tasty. This allows you to avoid vending machines and fast food at work or school.

Avoid Charging things you don't need, or Stress-Spending

If you had a bad week at work, it may be easy to decide to buy something just to reward yourself. But it's not a good idea. There are better ways to de-stress, like meditation or exercise. Even a nap can help. Working in the garden, watching movies or reading are great de-stressers that don't cost much, if anything.

Checking out Free or Cheap Programs offered by your Community

Most cities and towns have lots of events that are free. You may not have looked into them before. Check your city or county website or the library and get lists of upcoming events in the community. This will give you entertaining things you can do for free. You'll get free entertainment and sometimes even free meals.

Need to get out for some fresh air? Visit local parks, trails, tennis courts and basketball courts, if they're cheap or free. You can enjoy yourself for hours hiking or playing sports. Try new activities.

Cutting the Cord on your Cable

You can live without cable, although it will be an adjustment. The writer of this e-book does not have cable and has not for two years. Sure, there are things that would be fun to watch. But paying off debt is more important.

If you just can't let go of cable, at least cut out your premium packages. No one needs Cinemax, HBO and Starz. It's a lot cheaper to rent a movie now and then. Better yet, borrow movies on DVD from your library for free.

As long as you're cutting back on cable, cut back on the amount of time you and your family spend watching TV. How does this help you save money to pay down debt? You will have a lower electric bill, less exposure to ads that induce you to spend, and you can use the time, too, to focus on a home business or other money-making opportunities.

Signing up for Free Customer Rewards Programs

Regardless of where you live, you'll find many local retailers who offer rewards programs for shopping, when there are things you really need to buy. To maximize this type of program, create a separate email address just for their mailings, collect all the cards you can, and check that extra email account for coupons before you grocery shop.

Add to these discounts and rewards by using rewards-based credit cards (only if you can use them responsibly). These rewards can be redeemed for cash or other types of benefits.

Maintaining your Appliances

Check air filters in your furnace, etc, to ensure that they are not clogged with dust. Look behind large appliances and vacuum away dust. Check the vents on furnaces, air conditioners, dryers and refrigerators. If you have less dust, then you'll be allowing them to run more efficiently, which saves you money on utilities.

Making more Money = Paying off Debts Sooner

You can also pay more on your credit card balances if you make more money. This doesn't mean falling for those get-rich-quick internet schemes. There are legitimate ways to make extra money, online and offline.

Check to see which options might work for you, and charge prices that are comparable to others, if you are going to be offering a service.

1. Get another Brick and Mortar Job

This is the quickest way to make more money, right? It doesn't have to be another full time job. If you have extra time, you can turn it into extra money to pay on your debt.

2. Become a Freelancer

Freelancing allows you to make closer to what you make in your "real" job, since professional work usually pays more than work that is non-skilled. Use

LinkedIn or other online sites and find out how to get paid for the job skills you already have.

Freelance opportunities are abundant online and you can bid for freelance work at sites like Upwork. Understand what your work is worth and don't take the lowest paying jobs just because there is less competition.

3. Tutor

Whether you work with adults or high school age students, you can make money off any area in which you have expertise. You can do private tutoring or work with established groups like Kaplan. Plenty of students need help in their classes, and you can post your availability in schools and online. If you tutor adults, create a website or work with adult tutoring firms.

4. Coach

If you have a lot of experience in your field, you can coach others and help their careers. Set up a website or add to an existing site a section that describes what types of coaching you offer. Advertise your coaching in pertinent industry forums. Give new clients a first-time discount to sign up and refer others.

5. Blog

You probably have one area of business, technology or whatever in which you have a great deal of knowledge. Start a blog on this topic and use affiliate links and ads to generate money. It is essential to create content that is valuable to your audience, or you won't have enough traffic to make money. The idea is to become the go-to person in your field - a recognized expert.

6. Run Errands or do Handyman Work

If you'd rather let your brain relax in your second job, you can run errands for people or do odd jobs. Zaarly and TaskRabbit offer you chances to sign up. You can also put an ad on Craigslist. There are plenty of people out there who are not handy with tools or who have no time for errands. Capitalize on that.

These are some of the more unique ways you

can make extra money to pay down your credit card debt.

Conclusion

So…. Will it be better for you to pay off those smaller credit card balances first? Or hit the one with the highest APR?

The decision depends on you. If you need to see momentum more quickly, pay off the smaller balance first. This will keep you motivated. If you are a big-picture type of person, pay off the cards with higher interest first.

Don't forget the single more important thing that you need to help pay off your credit card debt sooner, not later – that skill is in understanding the difference between the things you WANT and the things you NEED.

We've included solid techniques on paying down debt and raising your credit score so you can get a car or a house if you want to.

We've also given you lots of other tips on cutting expenses, with those monies saved going toward paying off your credit card debt.

The next move is yours… Pay off those credit

cards and become debt-free!